D0997414

Pandas

Patricia Kendell

HODDER
Wayland

An imprint of Hodder Children's Books

Alligators Chimpanzees Dolphins Elephants
Gorillas Grizzly Bears Leopards Lions
Pandas Polar Bears Sharks Tigers

 © 2002 White-Thomson Publishing Ltd

Produced for Hodder Wayland by White-Thomson Publishing Ltd

Editor: Kay Barnham
Designer: Tim Mayer
Consultant: Stuart Chapman – International Conservation Officer,
  WWF-UK
Language Consultant: Norah Granger – Senior Lecturer in Primary
  Education at the University of Brighton
Picture research: Shelley Noronha – Glass Onion Pictures

Published in Great Britain in 2002 by Hodder Wayland,
an imprint of Hodder Children's Books.

Photograph acknowledgements:
Heather Angel 1 & 18, 3 (first, second & fourth), 4, 10, 11, 14,
15, 19, 21, 23, 24, 25, 29, 32;
Bruce Coleman Inc cover & 12 (Orion Press), 5, 16, 17;
Corbis 6, 7, 8 (Karen Su);
FLPA 3 (third), 13 (Sunset), 20 (Mark Newman), 22 (Gerard
Lacz), 28 (David Hosking);
Still Pictures 9 (Roland Seitre);
WWF-UK 26, 27 (Stuart Chapman).

British Library Cataloguing in Publication Data
Kendell, Patricia
  Pandas. - (In the wild)
  1. Pandas - Juvenile literature
  I. Title II. Barnham, Kay
  599.7'89

ISBN: 0 7502 4137 3

Printed and bound in Hong Kong

Hodder Children's Books
A division of Hodder Headline Limited
338 Euston Road, London NW1 3BH

Produced in association with WWF-UK.
WWF-UK registered charity number 1081247.
A company limited by guarantee number 4016725.
Panda device © 1986 WWF ® WWF registered trademark owner.

Contents

Where giant pandas live

Giant pandas live in the cool mountain forests of western China.

They belong to the bear family and are among the most **endangered** animals in the world.

5

Baby pandas

A mother panda usually has only one baby at a time. When it is born, the **cub** is tiny, helpless and weighs only 100-200 grammes.

Cubs are usually born in a **den** made in the hollow of a tree.

Looking after the cub

The cub drinks milk from its mother until it is one year old. Mother pandas lick their cubs clean.

This panda is cuddling her cub to keep it warm.

Keeping safe

Panda cubs are in danger from many different animals. The leopard is one of their enemies.

Cubs soon learn how to climb trees – away from
danger. Although adult pandas are big animals,
they are expert climbers.

Family life

A mother and cub make up a panda family.
They stay close together in their **territory**.

Cubs begin to eat bamboo leaves when they are
about eight months old. Their mothers teach
them where to find the best kind of bamboo.

Leaving home

A panda cub stays with its mother until it is two or three years old. Then it has to find a territory of its own.

Male pandas roam over a wide area.
They will fight with other males to win a **mate**.

Eating...

Pandas mainly eat bamboo. This panda is holding the bamboo and nibbling the juiciest parts.

When bamboo has grown flowers and turned
to seed, it dies. This panda will now have
to travel long distances to find new bamboo.

...and drinking

This panda has eaten a lot of juicy bamboo,
but it is still thirsty.

Pandas need to drink about twice a day.
They sometimes drink river water and
have been spotted licking snow.

Rest and play

Pandas spend up to 14 hours every day
searching for bamboo. After a good meal,
the panda has a rest.

Pandas sometimes roll in the snow. They do this for
fun and to clean their fur.

Keeping in touch

Pandas mainly live alone, but they do keep in touch with one another. Their low growls travel through the forest to other pandas.

They also leave **scent marks** and scratches on trees so other pandas know where they are.

Pandas in danger

Pandas are in great danger because much
of their forest home has been cut down
to make more space for people to live.

Towns and roads now divide up the forest.
This makes it more difficult for the shy panda
to move from one part of the forest to
another to find bamboo.

More dangers

There are laws to protect pandas. Some are killed for their fur. This cub is being taken to a safe place.

Some pandas are accidentally killed in traps set for other animals. These men will make sure that no more animals are caught in this trap.

Helping pandas to survive

Some people hoped that if pandas were safe in a zoo, they would have more cubs. Sadly this has not happened.

The best hope for pandas is to protect their forest homes
so that they are free to roam and have enough to eat.

Further information

Find out more about how we can help pandas in the future.

ORGANIZATIONS TO CONTACT

WWF-UK
Panda House, Weyside Park,
Godalming, Surrey GU7 1XR
Tel: 01483 426444
www.wwf.org.uk

American Museum of Natural History
Central Park West at 79th Street, New
York, NY 10024-5199, USA
Tel: 00212 769 5000
www.amnh.org

BOOKS

**Who am I? I am black and white,
big and bear-like and live in China:**
Moira Butterfield, Belitha Press 1998.

Bears and Pandas (Nature Watch):
Michael Bright, Lorenz Books 2000.

The Giant Panda – Hope for Tomorrow:
C A Amato and D Wenzel, Barrons
Juvenile 2000.

Giant Pandas (Wild World): Karen
Dudley, A&C Black 2000.

Giant Panda (Animals in Danger):
Rod Theodorou, Heinemann Library 2001.

Glossary

WEBSITES

Most young children will need adult help when visiting websites. Those listed have child-friendly pages to bookmark.

www.panda.org/kids/wildlife
WWF's virtual wildlife site has information about why the panda is endangered and what is being done to save it.

www.animal.discovery.com
This site includes a virtual journey to China called 'Meet the pandas'.

http://pandas.si.edu/kids
The Smithsonian site has a range of activities for young children including a quiz, crosswords and a 'Saving Great Pandas' activity book to download.

www.thebigzoo.com/Animals/
Giant_Panda.asp
This site has information about pandas with photographs and details of children's books.

cub – a young animal, in this case, a young panda.

den – a wild animal's home.

endangered – when there is a danger that all the animals of one kind, such as pandas, could die or be killed.

mate – to make babies.

scent marks – when pandas leave a special smell on a tree.

territory – the home area of an animal.

Index